101
QUIZZLERS

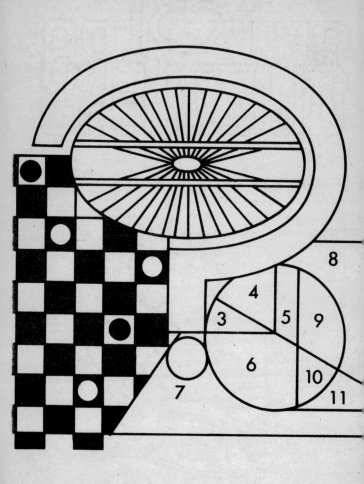

101 QUIZZLERS

Thomas Franklin
Illustrated by Jeremy Steele

Watermill Press
Mahwah, New Jersey

Published by: **Watermill Press**
               Mahwah, N.J.

ISBN 0-8167-1676-5

Copyright © 1989 Kidsbooks, Inc.

Manufactured in the United States of America

QUIZZLERS

1 Do you know the name of:

1 The bird that is a letter of the alphabet?
2 The bird that means to grumble?
3 The bird that is very quick?
4 The bird that means to shake with fright?
5 The bird that is a sailor's white uniform?
6 The bird that means to drink?
7 The bird that is very wise and knows it all?

7

2

Place eight checkers on a checker board so that no two checkers are in line. The checkers may not line up in a straight line — either horizontally, or vertically. Neither may they be lined up diagonally, or right across the board. Take a quick peek at the answer to get your clues, but flip right back to this page, or go right back to your board to work it out.

It sounds easy, but it's puzzling. You have exactly 64 squares on a checker board and only 8 checkers to place on them. That means there are 56 free squares left.

3

There are lots of ways to find a number someone else has thought of. Here is a very easy one.

First, ask someone to think of a number without giving you any hints or clues at all. Then ask the person to double the number. You then ask them to multiply that number by 5 and tell you what the new number is. You immediately tell them the number they first thought of. Just like that!

In the Answers section you can see how this Quizzler is done and read some examples. Once you know how the Quizzler works, you can probably work out even more astonishing examples of your ability to "read" your friends' minds.

4   What are the next numbers in this sequence, or row of numbers?

Clue: Think how you get from 2 to 4, from 4 to 8, and so on.

2, 4, 8, 10, 20, 22, ___, ___

5   Which of the following jumbled-up words is not a river?

Dunhos Trevese Zomana Sispimissip Line

6   Fill in the missing number. Use the same clues as above. How do you get from 2 to 3? from 3 to 5? And just keep on going.

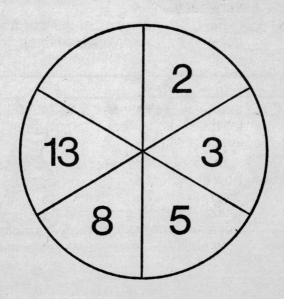

7

Here is a story told in pictures which are in the wrong order. Can you straighten them out?

8 Do you know what country makes these cars?

1 Mercedes; 2 Ferrari; 3 Skoda; 4 Volvo; 5 Citroen; 6 Rolls Royce; 7 Cadillac.

a Czechoslovakia; b Sweden; c America; d France; e England; f Germany; g Italy.

9 If you take all the consonants out of a word the results sometimes look very odd. Not only that, they would sound very strange. These words are names of countries in South America. What are the countries?

$$- - I - E \quad - - A - I -$$
$$U - U - U A -$$
$$A - - E - - I - A$$
$$- E - E - U E - A$$

10 In this sentence one letter of the alphabet has been left out every time it appears, and the words have all been run together. It looks like a code, but it's not. Can you replace the letter and read the sentence?

EEREALKINGDONAIDEPATH
AYHENESAAMANITH
AHEELBARRO.

11 A **satellite** is

   a a weapon used in war
   b a moon revolving around a planet
   c a kind of fizzy firework

12 An **arabesque** is

   a a circus horse
   b a lady from the East
   c a position in ballet

13 A **bassinet** is

   a a low musical instrument
   b a baby's cradle
   c a fisherman's tool

14 A **piccolo** is

   a a high-pitched wind instrument
   b a kind of ice cream drink
   c the word for baby in Italian

15 **Glucose** is

   a a kind of wood
   b sugar
   c an Oriental shawl

16 Arrange twelve matchsticks, or pretzels, or pencils — or anything straight — on a table as shown here.

What you need to do now is take away just *one* of the matchsticks, then move just *two* of them, and yet *leave only one on the table.* How is this impossible Quizzler done?

17 Johnny Appleseed wanted to plant a grove of apple trees. He was very particular. The trees had to be planted in nine straight rows and each row had to have five trees. He only had 19 seeds for trees.

How did his apple orchard grow? He did manage to plant nine straight rows and each of them had five trees.

18 Where are these spectacular mountain ranges?

1 Andes; **2** Atlas Mountains; **3** Rocky Mountains; **4** Himalayas; **5** Alps.

a Europe; **b** South America; **c** Africa; **d** North America; **e** Asia.

19

This happened years ago, way back when milkmen delivered milk and poured it out of old-fashioned containers for customers. But it's still a good Quizzler.

A milkman wanted to measure out 3 pints of milk from a large container and pour them into a can. However, he did not have a 3-pint size, and the customer insisted on exactly 3 pints, not a drop more, not a drop less. He did have a 10-pint, a 6-pint, and a 1-pint size.

Just how did he manage to measure 3 pints exactly — without using the 1-pint container three times and without wasting a drop of milk?

20 Some of the words and phrases in this story are in the wrong position. Can you find the words, or groups of words, and move them so that the story makes sense?

As I threw myself over the fence I was suddenly aware of the sound of a black bull behind me, and looking over my shoulder I saw huge pounding hooves charging toward me. I dashed for the field and immediately was walking across it into safety.

21 Here's another exciting animal story. All the words in each sentence are in the right order, but some of the sentences are not. Can you straighten them out?

One day Roger was walking in the country. As he passed near the edge of the cliffs he heard the whimper of a dog. There was no path up or down. He gently took the dog in his arms. Hurriedly Roger ran to the nearest farm. The farmer who lived there brought a rope. Peering cautiously over he saw a terrier clinging to the ledge eight yards below. The farmer and his helpers hauled them both back to safety. Fastening this around his waist, Roger was lowered over the edge.

22 Add the missing number to the triangle.

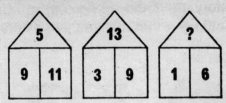

23 Which figure is the odd one out? Some-times Quizzlers are a bit simpler than you might suppose. Your clue: count.

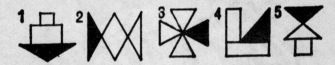

24 Which of these drawings is in the wrong order in this sequence? Clue: something is going on like clockwork.

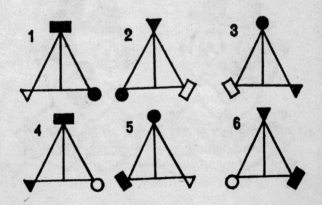

25

Which two clowns are the same? Only two are. There is something about the other six that makes them different.

26 What do these initials stand for? You've probably heard them and seen them, but what are they, and just what do they mean?

a PO   f MAYDAY

b JP   g ESP

c PS   h RSVP

d ASPCA   i LGM

e UFO   j ROGER

27 Many words sound the same although they are spelled differently, and some words are spelled almost the same but mean entirely different things. Can you pick out the right word in the following?

A bail/bale of straw is in the barn.

A peal/peel of thunder frightens some people.

A hoard/horde of treasure lies at the end of the passageway.

A broken down car is stationery/stationary.

I never go back on my word; it's a matter of principal/principle.

She must be physic/psychic if she can see ghosts.

28 Can you fill in the missing letters in the final word? Look at the first three very carefully. Isn't it strange they look very, very familiar?

y r a u n a j

y r a u r b e f

h c r a m

l _ _ _ a

29 What numbers go with the following?

1 a particularly unlucky Friday
2 Snow White
3 men carrying muskets
4 the oceans
5 a generous baker
6 an additional dimension
7 the senses

30 What are these strange things? Can you match their names with what they are?

1 goldenrod; 2 doe; 3 Rhode Island Red; 4 Portuguese Man O' War; 5 Man O' War.

a jellyfish; b hen; c flower; d famous race horse; e deer.

31 This is a tale of some children who long, long ago plotted night and day to escape from a high tower. They were terribly strong and extremely clever. They happened to be a princess and her younger brothers, two princes.

Every day their food was lifted up to them by a pulley. On the ends of the rope which passed over the pulley were two baskets. When one basket reached the ground, the other was right at their window. In their tower prison was an old cannonball which weighed 30 pounds. This gave them a clue. The princess weighed 90 pounds and the two princes weighed 50 pounds and 40 pounds. How could they use the cannonball to make an escape?

The princess said that if one basket were heavier, of course it would go down, but it could not be any more than 10 pounds heavier or else it would whiz down at a dangerous speed. The princes agreed that would be a problem.

Nevertheless they managed to make their escape, as astonishingly hard as it was to figure out. In fact it took them several days to plan their getaway. And, it took a lot of bravery and courage too.

32 In which sports are these words used?

1 home run; **2** birdie; **3** slalom; **4** puck; **5** love; **6** figure eight; **7** jump shot.

a skiing; **b** basketball; **c** badminton; **d** baseball; **e** tennis; **f** skating; **g** hockey.

33 In the following words the letters are mixed up. Can you sort them out? They are all school subjects.

a GOMETYRE   **b** TORHYIS

c CINSEEC   **d** BRAGALE

e SHINGLE

34 What arithmetic signs should go between the following numbers so that the answers come out right? Add, subtract, and multiply, and see if you come up with the correct answers.

a 4 5 7 3 = 13   **c** 1 4 4 = 8

b 4 3 7 = 49   **d** 21 3 8 24 = 842

e 6 7 11 5 = 29

35 The drawings below are in the right order from left to right — all except for one. Which drawing is not where it should be?

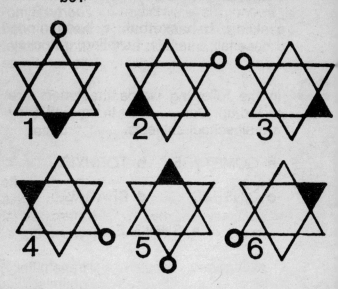

36 Arrange these drawings in the correct order. After drawing 1 comes drawing ? Clue: what would be drawing 5?

37 Have you ever thought of a word and then another just like it that has the exact same meaning? These words are synonyms. *Harsh* is a synonym for *cruel*, and *freedom* is a synonym for *liberty*. Synonyms are terrific to know when you need to supply a word in a crossword puzzle. Can you think of synonyms for these words?

bitter	tolerate	quiet
dry	shrill	mute

38 Antonyms are words with the opposite meanings. *Short* and *tall*, *big* and *small*, *friend* and *enemy*, are antonyms. What are the antonyms for these words?

exaggerate	repulsive	transmitter
silly	guest	optimist

39 Can you correct these sentences?

a A botanist predicts the future.
b A geologist studies plants.
c An astrologer has an unusual way of speaking.
d A clown examines rocks.
e A ventriloquist makes people laugh.

Which fairy is the odd one out?

41 A **buttress** is

a a female goat
b a projecting part of a wall
c a maid

42 A **terrapin** is

a a kind of tortoise
b a label for plants
c an antique bracelet

43 A **kimono** is

a a Chinese child
b a type of robe
c a flat-bottomed boat

44 A **mallard** is

a a pot for draining vegetables
b a perfumed ball
c a duck

45 A **possum** is

a a small furry animal
b a Dutch shoe
c a cooking pot

46 Make a magic cube! Magicians and wizards used to use a magic cube to help them cast spells. This one will cast a spell over you for awhile. After you get the cube made, each row of numbers that you write on the cube's squares must add up to exactly 194. Every single row, whether it's up and down, or across, or diagonal, must total 194! It may seem difficult, but don't give up.

To make the cube, copy this diagram onto a light piece of cardboard. After cutting it out, bend the cardboard along the dotted lines. It will fold easily into a small cube. Finish the cube by pasting the "Paste Here" edges, or use Scotch tape.

Now for the hard part — the numbers. Each side of the cube has 16 squares on it, and since there are 6 sides, you have 96 squares to fill. To make things easier, you may only use the numbers 1 through 96 to fill in the squares. But remember, every single line on each side of the cube must add up to 194.

There is a method! One clue to begin with is to divide the numbers into groups of low numbers and high numbers. It would be impossible to jot down numbers and come up with the correct totals for every single line. Once you have discovered the trick with numbers in the Answer section, use it to write the numbers on your cube. You will have a magic cube to baffle your friends with, and perhaps cast a few spells.

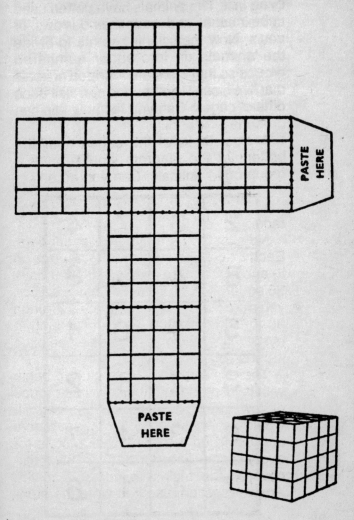

47 Here is a diagram of animal cages in a scientist's laboratory. Each square within the rectangle has a group of animals living in it. The animals have gotten used to their cages and made their burrows, or nests. Now the scientist wants to divide the animals up into *equal* numbered groups so that there are fourteen animals that live close together and can visit each others' cages. Can you tell how this can be done?

A clue: three of the cages near the bottom of the diagram would make a group of 14 animals. Can you go on?

2	3	7	4
8	4	3	8
5	1	10	4
3	2	8	2
6	3	4	7
7	4	1	6

48 You can do this trick almost anywhere. All you need is a clock.

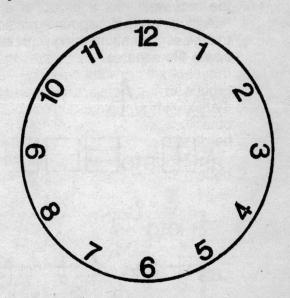

First, ask a friend to think of a number on the clock's dial.

Then tell your friend you will point to several of the numbers. What he or she must do is to add a 1 to the number they *thought* of every time you point — but only up until their numbers add up to 20. Then they must call out "Stop."

Tell your friend that you will always be pointing to the number they thought of when they tell you to stop. How is it done? Not by magic, but quite easily once you learn the Quizzler.

49

Can you complete the following "sentences"? Select the number you think is the "answer."

A clue: what is happening inside the triangles? The same thing must happen inside the squares.

50 The numbers in each of these diagrams all follow the same pattern. Can you fill in the missing ones?

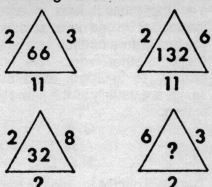

51 What would you do with these things?

1 mallet; **2** outrigger; **3** casserole; **4** musket; **5** carousel; **6** metronome; **7** Cheddar.

a eat it; **b** fire it; **c** pound with it; **d** sail it; **e** ride on it; **f** count with it; **g** cook in it.

52 What rivers flow in these cities?

1 St. Louis; **2** Vienna; **3** London; **4** New York; **5** Cairo.

a Danube; **b** Nile; **c** Missouri; **d** Hudson; **e** Thames.

53 An acrostic is a kind of crossword puzzle — a special kind. It is an arrangement of words with another word hidden in them. The most usual kind of acrostic is a vertical, or up and down acrostic, in which the first letters of each word, read down, make another word. This is not very difficult to arrange, even though the words are usually all the same length. For instance:

```
C A R
A N T
T O E
```

The word cat CAT is hidden here. But in a good acrostic the hidden word should have some kind of relation to all the other words. A much better acrostic of CAT would be this:

```
C L A W S
A L L E Y
T I G E R
```

Cats have claws; an alley cat is a street cat; and a tiger is a larger member of the cat family.

Now see if you can solve this acrostic:

a					
b					
c					
d					

a a large piece of luggage
b the part of the tree that grows in the
  ground
c a person who is older
d the name of this planet

And here is another of the same kind of acrostic:

a a small body orbiting a planet
b this makes distant objects appear
  larger
c the study of other worlds
d a piece of uranium gives this off

54 Here is a double acrostic. Both the first and the last letters of each word, read downward, make two more words:

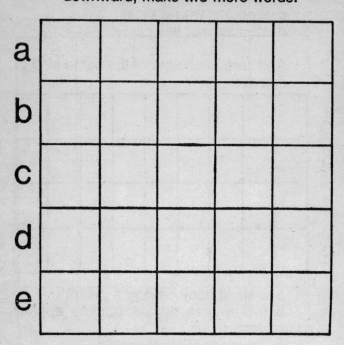

a   what to do with a gun

b   an instrument for making wood smooth

c   a book of maps

d   a "star" with a long tail

e   stories of fantastic achievements

55 And here is a diagonal acrostic. The hidden word is read diagonally from the top left to the bottom right:

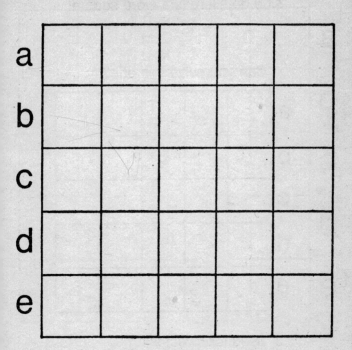

a a person who trains athletes
b first or highest
c old-fashioned weapon
d many people gathered together
e often married to a king

56 A word square is an arrangement of words that read the same both down and across — that is, the letters on the outside do. Here is a word square:

P E N
E M U
N U T

Can you solve this one?

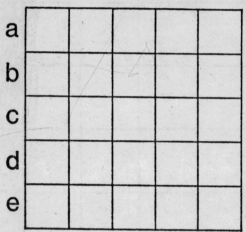

a used for sweetening
b the act of using
c high winds
d one who acts for another
e pauses from work

Try making up some acrostics and word squares yourself. Start with the word squares first and work up to acrostics.

57 Which lizard is the longer one? Look carefully.

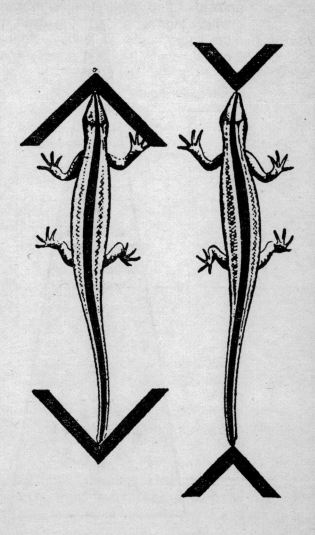

58

Now that you've looked at the lizard, which oval is the larger one?

Turn the book around and look at the ovals more than one way.

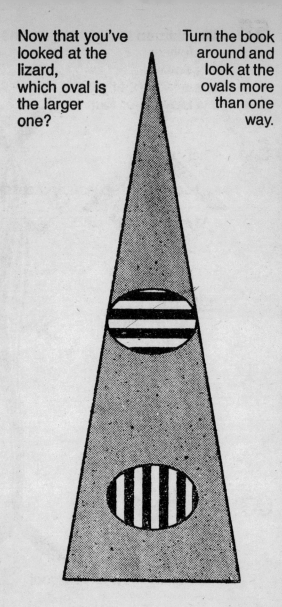

59 A **cyclamen** is

   a a flower
   b a period of fifty years
   c a bicycle for four

60 A **carousel** is

   a a dealer in second-hand cars
   b a four-part song
   c a merry-go-round

61 A **talisman** is

   a a lucky charm
   b a flying carpet
   c a sailor's hat

62 A **bassoon** is

   a a chess piece
   b worn with a kilt
   c a musical instrument

63 A **spatula** is

   a a type of footwear
   b a flat spoon
   c a rapidly moving whirlpool

64 A lady who did not want her age known once gave this answer to the question "How old are you?"

"I have nine children. All of my children were born three years apart. I was nineteen years old when my first child was born, and my youngest is now the same age. I *never* tell my age."

What was the lady's age? It can be figured out! She never tells her age, yet she does tell it — in a roundabout way.

65 Can you draw the missing figure in the third row?

66 Sports Quizzlers:

1 What sport uses a shuttlecock?
2 In what sport do you score a touchdown?
3 In what sport do you ride horses?
4 Billie Jean King plays this sport.
5 What is an Olympiad?
6 What game do you play with a mallet?
7 Who was the first athlete to run a mile in less than four minutes?
8 In which sport do you use a puck?

67 Here is a super-tricky Quizzler:

A certain three-figure number when halved becomes zero. Can you find the magic number and solve this Quizzler?

68 Reasonable Quizzlers:

You know that oranges are cheaper than grapefruit, and grapefruit cost less than pomegranates. Are pomegranates more expensive than oranges?

Someone has told you that Philip has eight books, Paul has half as many again, and Peter has twice as many as Paul. How many more books does Peter have than Philip?

Can you see the gray spots?

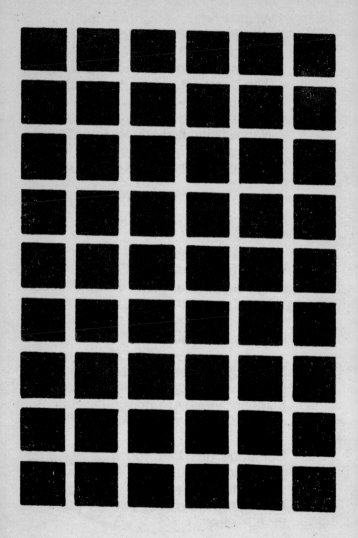

70 Are you looking at one candlestick, or two faces?

71 Are lines going straight across the oval parallel to each other, just like railroad tracks? Look hard, and look again.

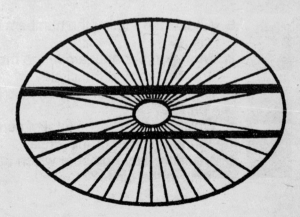

72

Look carefully at this drawing, and then see how many of the questions you can answer.

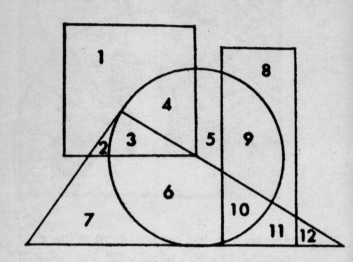

a What is the total of the numbers in the circle?

b What number appears in the triangle, the square and the circle?

c What is the total of the numbers in the triangle?

d Which is more — the total of numbers in the triangle, or the circle?

e Are there any numbers which appear only in the circle?

73 Starting at 1 and going clockwise around the circle the numbers are really what you might expect. Can you fill in the missing number?

74 What do 111, 222, and 333 have in common beside the fact they are repeating numbers *and* three-figure numbers?

There is a "magic" number which, if multiplied by 3, 6, 9, 12, 15, 18, 21, 24, and 27 equals 111, 222, 333 etc. — all the way up to 999!

What is the magic number?

75 A **pecan** is

a a soft drink
b a bird with a large beak
c a nut

76 A **dromedary** is

a a drummer
b a type of camel
c a droning bee

77 An **artichoke** is

a an attractive necklace
b a vegetable
c a set of handcuffs

78 A **flapjack** is

a a loose kind of shoe
b a thick pancake
c someone who repairs high buildings

79 A **taxidermist** is

a someone who stuffs animals
b a fortune teller
c a student taxi driver

80 It's always useful to know about inventions. Do you know:

1 Who invented dynamite?
2 What Madame Curie discovered?
3 When the first postage stamp was used?
4 Who spoke the first words on a telephone?

81 Did you know these facts about planes, trains, and cars?

1 An aircraft with a propeller on top is called what?
2 A green-colored vehicle used by the army is what?
3 Who first flew alone across the ocean?
4 Train engines used to run on this.

82 Choose from the words in parentheses, the one that is opposite (or nearly opposite) in meaning. For example: SLOPE (slant, level) — the answer is level.

a EMPTY (nothing, vacant, full, hungry)
b FLOAT (wood, paper, lift, sink, swim)
c LOVE (cherish, enemy, hate, friend)
d LIQUID (water, gas, solid, ice)
e BITTER (sweet, salt, sour, acid)

Study these two pages for three minutes, and then close the book. How many of the objects can you remember?

84

Here is an alphabet Quizzler. Substitute your words for the clues given. The first word will begin with A, the second with B, and so on.

a a book of maps
b a tropical fruit
c the little god of love
d a dark brown, sticky fruit
e what the chicken lays
f it burns
g a moving mass of ice
h a game played with a puck
i a wall-clinging plant
j the bone that moves your mouth
k you use it in a lock
l it allows us to speak to one another
m small animal
n a coin
o it pushes the boat along
p the opposite of war
q a liquid metal
r old pieces of cloth
s opposite of sweet
t something to aim at
u a type of clothing
v his day is the 14th of February
w talk very softly
x a musical instrument
y three feet
z it is very cold when a thermometer registers this

85 Try this super-puzzling Quizzler.

The letters A, B, C, D, and E are scrambled up with the numbers 1, 2, 3, 4, and 5. Can you match each letter with its number?

Here are the facts:
   A is an even number.
   B is neither 3 nor 1.
   C is 3.
   D is either 2 or 3.

86 What are these instruments used for?

   barometer   thermometer

   cyclometer   metronome

             abacus

87 How many words do you know that end with "scope?" There are dozens. Start a list and count them.

88

Do you know the answers to the questions "Where?" and "What?"

1 What is the lowest valley in the USA?
2 Is Alaska part of the United States?
3 What is the capital of Brazil?
4 Which state is called the Bluegrass State?
5 What is the highest mountain in the world?
6 Where is the Aswan Dam?
7 What is the capital of Canada?
8 What are the names of the five great lakes between Canada and the United States?

89

If you really like to explore and are adventurous you might know or want to know:

1 What is the Northwest Passage?
2 Is there any land at the North Pole?
3 Who first sailed alone around the world?
4 Who was murdered in the Sandwich Islands in 1779?

The letters of the alphabet are fascinating — and beautiful. Take a good look at them before you answer these questions.

a How many letters have a curve in them?
b Name five curved letters that are grouped next to each other.
c How many letters look the same in a mirror?

A B C D E

F G H I J

K L M N O

P Q R S T

U V W

X Y Z

91 Match the words with the phrases below
which describe them.

1 punctuality; **2** generous; **3** hasty;
4 seldom; **5** glare; **6** gorge.

a look at something fixedly
b do things in a hurried fashion
c not very often
d eat a large quantity
e arriving exactly on time
f giving freely

92 Some people make a hobby of bridges.
They know everything about them, just
like other people know railroads. Here
are some questions about bridges.

1 Where is the Bridge of Sighs?
2 Where is the Golden Gate Bridge?
3 What is an aqueduct?
4 What is a "swing" bridge?
5 What two countries are linked by the
    Rainbow Bridge, and where is it?

93 Here is a Quizzler all about food.

1 What is a cantaloupe?
2 How does a pineapple grow?
3 What is spaghetti made from?
4 What is a Welsh Rabbit?
5 What are Parmesan, Gouda, and Edam?
6 What can saccharine be used instead of?
7 Is a lobster really red when it is alive?

94 Now for the buildings expert.

1 Where is the Taj Mahal?
2 Who lives in the White House?
3 How many floors has the Empire State Building?
4 What is the tallest building in Chicago?
5 What is the name of the most famous building on the Acropolis in Athens, Greece?

95 How do 5 and 5 make 11?

Did you know that you can count to eleven on ten fingers?

It's ridiculous, but here's how:

You begin with the thumb of your left hand and count all the fingers of both hands. "One, two, three, four, five, six, seven, eight, nine, ten."

Then begin with your right thumb and count back. "Ten, nine, eight, seven, six." (The sixth is your little finger.)

You then hold up your left hand with the fingers spread out and say, "And five makes eleven."

Can you explain this?

96 In each of these lists there is a word that does not really belong. Can you pick these words out?

a Holland, Russia, Spain, Italy, Asia
b football, hockey, tennis, baseball
c daisy, pansy, violin, carnation

97 In each of these sentences the two missing words are the reverse of each other, such as TUB and BUT. Can you fill in the blanks?

a The ____ burst and the water rushed like ____ down the hill.

b The day I ____ her ____ the happiest day of my life.

98 How do you get from HOME to SALT in four easy steps?

Word changing step-by-step is a fascinating puzzle. The idea is to go from one word to another of the same length, changing one letter each time, and making a real word with each step. For instance, you can change THE to SEA in three steps:

SHE — Take out the T and add S.
SEE — Take out the H and add E.
SEA — Remove the final E and add an A.

Now try HOME to SALT.

99 Try this out on your friends.

Get a sheet of paper and a pencil.

Ask a friend to write down any five-figure number. Suppose your friend writes

7 8 9 5 6.

Take back the paper, memorize the five figures, and write something on the other side without letting your friend see what it is.

After turning the paper over with the original side up, hand it back to your friend and ask that five more figures be written under those that were first written down.

Suppose now that your friend writes

4 3 9 8 7.

You then say, "I will add a few more," and quick as a wink write

5 6 0 1 2.

You again offer the paper to your friend who writes

7 3 6 8 4 this time.
You add 2 6 3 1 5

Now you have five numbers down. You hand the sheet to your friend to do the additions. They are:

```
  7 8 9 5 6
  4 3 9 8 7
  5 6 0 1 2
  7 3 6 8 4
  2 6 3 1 5
─────────────
2 7 8 9 5 4
```

Now ask your friend to turn the paper over. Imagine your friend's surprise to find the number

2 7 8 9 5 4

You have written the answer before the figures were even written down. Not only did you "read" your friend's mind, but you predicted what a five-figure addition would turn out to be way before some of the figures were thought of.

How is it done? See the Answers.

100 Old-fashioned murder mysteries are the best, say murder mystery fans. In this one the setting is a castle; the witness is the butler; and the corpse is that of the incredibly wealthy owner of the castle.

Read the story and then tell how the detective knew the butler was lying.

The butler found the body and immediately sent for the police. The Inspector questioned him and this was the butler's story: "I left him at 3 p.m., sitting before a cozy fire in the library. When I returned at 6 p.m., I glanced through the library window and saw that he was talking to someone. I could not see into the room as the frost had covered the panes, but I scraped away the ice with my knife so as to see more clearly. Before I could move, the stranger shot him and then rushed away. I telephoned the police as soon as I got in."

101 A **will o' the wisp** is

    a a veil
    b something you can't quite see
    c a type of wasp

ANSWERS

1 1 jay; **2** grouse; **3** swift; **4** quail; **5** duck; **6** swallow; **7** the *wise* owl, of course.

The pictures are of the jay, grouse, swallow, owl, duck, swift, and quail. Start with the jay in the upper left-hand corner of the page and "read" clockwise.

2 Here is one way you might have set up your checker board. There are others, too. Check to make sure that none of your checkers are in line. Then try to find some other ways to solve this Quizzler and have some more fun.

3 Suppose your friend thought of the number 7. When 7 is doubled it becomes 14. Multiplying 14 by 5, the result is 70. To get the "answer," you drop the zero and tell your friend, "7!"

Here is another example, just to prove the Quizzler works for other numbers. Take 8 and double it. Then multiply 16 by 5. This equals 80, and you have the answer — 8.

Of course this is a very simple trick. If you do it more than once with the same person they may see through it.

4 44, 46. The Method: Add 2 to the first number, then multiply by 2, and so on. The clue is 2. First you add 2, then you multiply by 2.

5 Trevese, or Everest, is not a river.

The rivers are the Hudson, Amazon, Mississippi, and Nile.

6 21. The Method: Here 2 is added to the next number, 3, to get the third number, 5. So....8 added to 13 equals 21.

7 The right order is C A D F B E.

8 If you matched cars and countries up like this you were right:

1 -f; 2 - g; 3 - a; 4 - b; 5 - d; 6 - e; 7 - c.

The Mercedes is made in Germany.
The Ferrari is an Italian car.
The Skoda comes from Czechoslovakia.
The Volvo is a Swedish car.
The Citroen is made in France.
The Rolls Royce is an English car.
The Cadillac is made in America.

9 The countries in South America are:

CHILE   BRAZIL
URUGUAY
ARGENTINA
VENEZUELA

10 W is the missing letter. When you place the W into the message it reads:

WEWEREWALKINGDOWNAWIDEPATH
WAYWHENWESAWAMANWITH
AWHEELBARROW

The message is easily read now:
We were walking down a wide pathway when we saw a man with a wheelbarrow.

11 b

12 c

12 b

14 a

15 b

16 Here is the solution to the trick. The stick you remove is from the center square. You then move two others, one in the center square slanting down, and one in the third square.

Maybe you didn't expect this kind of a "one!"

17 The diagram below shows how the trees were planted. The dots are trees. The rows were *straight but not parallel!*

If you don't believe that there are nine rows, just count them out starting from the upper right going clockwise. There are three rows of trees starting from this point.

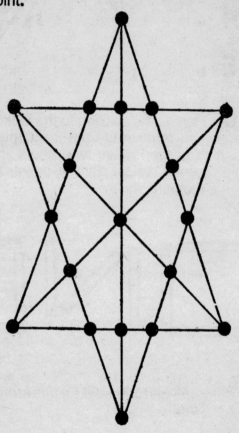

18 Here are the correct match-ups.

1 - b; 2 - c; 3 - d; 4 - e; 5 - a.

19 The milkman was a genius, and a whiz at on-the-spot solutions to difficult problems.

What did he do? He filled the 10-pint can with milk right up to the 10-pint mark. Then he filled the 6-pint can and the 1-pint can, leaving exactly 3 pints in his 10-pint can!

20 Moving a word or a few words here and there, the black bull story makes much better sense. Here it is:

As I *was walking across* the *field* I was suddenly aware of the sound of *pounding hooves* behind me, and looking over my shoulder I saw a huge *black bull* charging toward me. I dashed for the *fence* and immediately *threw myself over it* into safety.

21 Here is the rescue story just as it happened.

One day Roger was walking in the country. As he passed near the edge of the cliffs he heard the whimper of a dog. Peering cautiously over he saw a terrier clinging to the ledge eight yards below. There was no path up or down. Hurriedly Roger ran to the nearest farm. The farmer who lived there brought a rope. Fastening this around his waist, Roger was lowered over the edge. He gently took the dog in his arms. The farmer and his helpers hauled them both to safety.

22 18. The Method: Each set of numbers adds up to 25.

23 3. 3 is the odd one out because all of the other designs and shapes consist of three shapes. Number 3 is made up of four different shapes.

24 If you used the clockwork method you would have seen that 5 and 6 should be switched. The shapes on the points of the triangle should move around clockwise.

25 Yes, these clowns do take a while to study. No, it isn't the shape of the shine on the clowns' noses or the reflections on their black hats. There are more important differences.

But first, the clown on the bottom right-hand corner of page 18 and the top right-hand corner of page 19 are practically identical twins. Here's what makes the others different:

On page 18, the upper left-hand corner clown's bowtie lacks a stripe.

Somehow the clown on the upper right-hand corner forgot to pencil in the wrinkle line from his round nose to the corner of his lips.

The lower left-hand clown is missing a sprig of hair above his ear.

On page 19, the upper left-hand clown was careless with his make-up. His right eye is unfinished.

The clown on the lower left forgot to paste on his chin whiskers.

And finally, the clown on the lower right doesn't have a shiny black nose!

26 Here are the meanings of the initials everyone needs to know.

a Post Office
b Justice of the Peace
c Post Script — what you add to a letter after the "script," or writing
d American Society for the Prevention of Cruelty to Animals
e Unidentified Flying Objects
f International distress signal — SOS
g Extra-sensory Perception — our sixth sense
h On an invitation this means "Please reply."
i Little Green Men — what science fiction writers write about
j "Message received"

27 The words which sound or look the same should be:

bale — peal — hoard — stationary — principle — psychic

28 The missing letters are i, r, and p. If you read January backward on the first line, then February, and March, you can certainly add an i, r, p to the letters on the last line and come up with the correct answer, April.

29
1 Friday the 13th
2 Snow White and the Seven Dwarfs
3 The Three Musketeers
4 The Seven Seas
5 a baker's dozen of thirteen
6 the fourth dimension
7 the five senses

30 1 - c; 2 - e; 3 - b; 4 - a; 5 - d.

31 Here is how the princess and her two brothers plotted their escape.

First, the smallest prince went down using the cannonball as a counterweight. (He only weighed 10 pounds more than the cannonball.) Second, the cannonball was taken out of the basket and the older prince stepped in, while the younger prince went up again, acting as counterweight. (The princes' weights were only 10 pounds different.)

Next the cannonball went down alone. The older prince who was on the ground stepped into the basket along with the cannonball, allowing the princess to come down to the ground. (She weighed only 10 pounds more than the cannonball and the oldest prince.) Again the cannonball went down alone.

Next the youngest prince went down

and up again as a counterweight for his older brother. Now both the oldest prince and the princess were on the ground.

And finally, how did the littlest prince get down? He lowered himself by the rope!

32 1 - d; 2 - c; 3 - a; 4 - g; 5 - e ; 6 - f; 7 - b.

33 The subjects are:

a GEOMETRY   c HISTORY
b SCIENCE   d ALGEBRA
      e ENGLISH

34
a 4 + 5 + 7 - 3 = 13
b 4 plus 3 makes 7; 7 times 7 = 49
c 1 times 4 is 4; then add on 4 = 8
d 21 - 3 + 824 = 842
e 6 + 7 + 11 + 5 = 29

35 The third drawing should be at the end of the line so that the sequence of drawings is 1, 2, 4, 5, 6, 3. The black triangle and the circle move around the points of the star in a clockwise direction.

36 1, 4, 2, 5, 3. This shape gets blacker and blacker and blacker.

37 The answers are:

bitter/acid   shrill/piercing
dry/arid   quiet/stillness
tolerate/permit   mute/silent

There are really lots of synonyms. You might have used *allow* or *endure* for tolerate and been quite right.

38 Here are the antonyms, or opposites.

exaggerate/minimize   guest/host
silly/serious   transmitter/receiver
repulsive/attractive   optimist/pessimist

Just like synonyms, there are other opposites. For instance, another one for *silly* would be *reasonable*.

39 a A botanist studies plants.
b A geologist examines rocks.
c An astrologer predicts the future.
d A clown makes people laugh.
e A ventriloquist has an unusual way of speaking.

40 The third fairy has lost her shoe.

41 b

42 a

43 b

44 c

45 a

46 As each side of the cube has 16 squares, the secret is to write 8 low numbers and 8 high numbers on each side. If these are arranged as follows, the total of the numbers on each side of the cube will be the same:

1-8	and	89-96
9-16		81-88
17-24		73-80
25-32		65-72
33-40		57-64
41-48		49-56

Now all you have to do is to arrange these numbers on each side of the cube according to the rules in Quizzlers. See if you can do it, and then look at the diagram to make sure you have done it correctly.

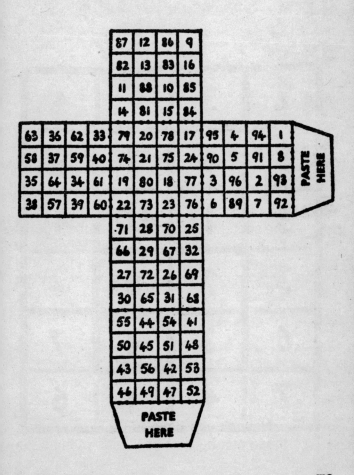

47 The heavy lines show how the animals' cages were separated. Every group of three side-by-side cages has 14 animals in it.

2	3	7	4
8	4	3	8
5	1	10	4
3	2	8	2
6	3	4	7
7	4	1	6

48 The first seven numbers you point to may be any numbers on the dial. For example, first point to 3, then 9, then 6, then 4, then 11, then 2, then 8.

However, the eighth number you point must be 12. You then go backward until your friend calls out "Stop," (from 12, to 11, to 10, to 9, to 8, and so on).

You then tell your friend that the number you are pointing at is the original number thought of, and it always is! It always will be!

Example: Suppose your friend thinks of 4. You first point to any seven numbers, while he or she mentally adds one for each number. That brings them to 11 (4, the number thought of, plus 7).

The eighth number you point to is 12; your ninth is 11; your tenth is 10; your next, 9; your next, 8; your next, 7; your next 6; your next, 5; your next 4.

Your friend has been counting all the time, and when you reach 4, his or her count reaches 20 and you hear the "Stop" signal.

You are then pointing at the number your friend originally thought of — 4!

49 a - 3; b - 2; c - 1; d - 2.

50 2 and 36. The Method: The three numbers outside the triangles are multiplied together to give the number inside.

51 1 - c; 2 - d; 3 - g; 4 - b; 5 - e; 6 - f; 7 - a.

52 1 - c; 2 - a; 3 - e; 4 - d; 5 - b. .

T	R	U	N	K
R	O	O	T	S
E	L	D	E	R
E	A	R	T	H

S	A	T	E	L	L	I	T	E
T	E	L	E	S	C	O	P	E
A	S	T	R	O	N	O	M	Y
R	A	D	I	A	T	I	O	N

a	S	H	O	O	T
b	P	L	A	N	E
c	A	T	L	A	S
d	C	O	M	E	T
e	E	P	I	C	S

a what to do with a gun
b an instrument for making wood smooth
c a book of maps
d a "star" with a long tail
e stories of fantastic acheivements

a	C	O	A	C	H
b	P	R	I	M	E
c	S	W	O	R	D
d	C	R	O	W	D
e	Q	U	E	E	N

- **a** a person who trains athletes
- **b** first or highest
- **c** old-fashioned weapon
- **d** many people gathered together
- **e** often married to a king

a S	U	G	A	R
b U	S	A	G	E
c G	A	L	E	S
d A	G	E	N	T
e R	E	S	T	S

a used for sweetening
b the act of using
c high winds
d one who acts for another
e pauses from work

57 Both lizards are the same length!

58 The ovals are the same size in spite of what you might have thought! Your eyes can play tricks on you.

59 a

60 c

61 a

62 c

63 b

64 The lady who would not tell her age was 19 when her oldest child was born and 43 when her youngest child was born. The length of time between her first and last children has to be 24 because there were three years between them all. Add 24 to 19 and you get 43. Then add another 19 to include the years since her youngest child was born. The lady is 62 years old!

65 The missing figure should have a square head, a round body, one finger on each hand, and one toe on each foot to make it just right for the sequence.

66
1 Badminton
2 Football
3 Polo
4 Tennis
5 The four-year period between Olympic Games
6 Croquet
7 Roger Bannister in May, 1954
8 Hockey

67 If the number 888 is halved, as shown here, it becomes zero.

$$888 = \overline{888} = 0$$

68 Answer to the first Reasonable Quizzler: yes.
Answer to the second Reasonable Quizzler: 16.

Since Paul has 12 books (Phillip's eight and half again), twice Paul's books are 24. Then Peter has 16 more books than Phillip.

69 You should be able to see the gray spots, in fact you can hardly *not* see the gray spots.

70 If you stare at the picture, sometimes you see a candlestick and sometimes two faces in profile.

71 The lines are parallel.

72 a 37; b 3; c 51; d the triangle, as the circle has only 37; e yes — 5.

73 243. The Method: The first figure, 1, is multiplied by the next — 3, and the result is 3; then 3 is multiplied by 3 to give 9; then 9 by 3 to give 27; and 9 by 27 = 243.

74 The magic number is 37.

$$37 \times 3 = 111$$
$$37 \times 6 = 222$$
$$37 \times 9 = 333$$
$$37 \times 12 = 444$$
$$37 \times 15 = 555$$
$$37 \times 18 = 666$$
$$37 \times 21 = 777$$
$$37 \times 24 = 888$$
$$37 \times 27 = 999$$

75 c

76 b

77 b

78 b

79 a

80 1 Dr. Alfred Nobel; 2 Radium; 3 May 6, 1840; 4 Alexander Graham Bell.

81 1 helicopter; 2 jeep; 3 Charles Lindbergh; 4 steam.

82 a full; b sink; c hate; d solid; e sweet.

83 How many of the objects did you remember? Perhaps you started with the owl. But did you remember the spectacles, the rubber band, the needle, the candy?

Try this Quizzler a second time and see just how much more you remember.

84

A	atlas	N	nickel
B	banana	O	oar
C	cupid	P	peace
D	date	Q	quicksilver
E	egg	R	rags
F	fire	S	sour
G	glacier	T	target
H	hockey	U	uniform
I	ivy	V	(St.) Valentine
J	jawbone	W	whisper
K	key	X	xylophone
L	language	Y	yard
M	mouse	Z	zero

85

A is 4; B is 5; C is 3; D is 2; E is 1.

You figure it out this way:

Your first fact is that C is 3.

D has to be 2 because it is either 2 or 3 and C is 3.

Since A is an even number, it can only be 4 (the other remaining numbers are 1 and 5).

B is not 1 (B is neither 3 nor 1), so it has to be 5.

This leaves E as the only possible number 1.

86 A barometer measures the pressure of air; a thermometer measures the temperature; a cyclometer measures the number of miles travelled on a bicycle; a metronome gives the beat in music; an abacus is a simple calculator.

87 The most important "scope" words are: telescope, microscope, horoscope, bioscope, kaleidoscope, periscope, gyroscope, hydroscope.

88 1 Death Valley; 2 yes; 3 Brasilia; 4 Kentucky; 5 Mount Everest; 6 Egypt; 7 Ottawa; 8 Superior, Michigan, Huron, Erie, and Ontario.

89 1 a sea route from the Atlantic to the Pacific through the Arctic seas; 2 no — only ice; 3 Captain Joshua Slocum in 1898; 4 Captain Cook.

90 a eleven letters
b O P Q R S
c A H I M O T U V W X Y

91 1 - e; 2 - f; 3 - b; 4 - c; 5 - a; 6 - d.

92 1 Venice; 2 San Francisco; 3 a bridge carrying a canal; 4 a bridge in which a section swings to one side to allow free passage to ships on a canal or river; 5 Rainbow Bridge crosses the Niagara River and links Canada and the USA.

93 1 a type of melon; 2 on a low bush about a yard tall; 3 a dough made from hard wheat; 4 cheese and milk on toast; 5 types of cheese; 6 sugar; 7 no—green.

94 1 India; 2 President of the United States; 3 102; 4 Sears Tower; 5 the Parthenon.

95 The strange result comes from changing from subtraction to addition. You are asking your friend to subtract down to six, then add on five, which makes eleven. You are suddenly switching from sub-traction to addition.

It's just one of those Quizzlers that puzzle other people for a while. Only try it once, and don't explain.

96 **a** Asia is a continent — the others are countries; **b** hockey uses a puck, not a ball; **c** violin is a musical instrument — the others are flowers.

97 **a** The dam burst and the water rushed like mad down the hill.

b The day I saw her was the happiest day of my life.

98 Here is how you make these hops.

First HOME.
Substitute an S, and you get SOME.
Slip in an L and you get SOLE.
Try an A and you get SALE.
Now all you need is that T to make SALT.

99 The number your friend first wrote was: 78956

When you write something on the reverse side of the paper, all you have to do is to reduce the last number (in this case a 6) by 2, and place a 2 in front of the first number written (in this case a 7). What you write on the back of the paper is 278954.

Your friend then writes five more figures. 43987

You add five more, in each case making your friend's number added to yours equal to 9. That is, you write 56012
($4+5=9$, $3+6=9$, $9+0=9$, $8+1=9$, $7+2=9$).

Your friend adds five more 73684 and you again add five, making the two figures add up to 9 in each case. 26315

This gives the total which is already written on the back of your paper. 278954

This Quizzler is guaranteed to work — no matter what numbers are given to you. Only you must be quick about adding up to 9.

100 Frost does not form on the outside of a window, but on the inside. This important clue immediately alerted the detective to the fact something was quite wrong with the butler's story.

101 b